"For us, everything is memory; it's part of our heritage. We have no written language. Our songs, our prayers, our stories, they're all handed down from grandfather to father to children—we listen, we hear, we learn to remember everything."

Carl Gorman, Navajo Code Talker

Text copyright © 2016 by J. Patrick Lewis   Illustrations copyright © 2016 by Gary Kelley

Edited by Kate Riggs   Designed by Rita Marshall, with Gary Kelley

Published in 2016 by Creative Editions   P.O. Box 227, Mankato, MN 56002 USA

Creative Editions is an imprint of The Creative Company   www.thecreativecompany.us

Printed in China

Library of Congress Cataloging-in-Publication Data

Lewis, J. Patrick. / Kelley, Gary, illustrator.

The Navajo Code Talkers / by J. Patrick Lewis; illustrated by Gary Kelley.

Summary: Amidst a complicated history of mistreatment by and distrust of the

American government, the Navajo people—especially bilingual code

talkers—helped the Allies win World War II.

Identifiers: LCCN 2015048108 / ISBN 978-1-56846-295-0

Subjects: LCSH: World War, 1939-1945—Cryptography—Juvenile literature.

World War, 1939-1945—Participation, Indian—Juvenile literature. / Navajo language—Juvenile literature.

Navajo code talkers—Juvenile literature. / Navajo Indians—History—20th century—Juvenile literature.

United States. Marine Corps—Indian troops—Juvenile literature.

Classification: D810.C88 L495 2016 / 940.54 / 59730899726—dc23

First edition 9 8 7 6 5 4 3 2 1

J. PATRICK LEWIS + GARY KELLEY

THE NAVAJO CODE TALKERS

Creative Editions

DOWN the long vista of years, the Navajo, who called themselves *Diné* ("The People"), were bound to each other and to their tribal land—the Four Corners of Colorado, New Mexico, Arizona, and Utah—otherwise known as *Dinétah* ("Navajo Land").

FOR decades, they had defended Dinétah, their grandchildren, and their children until the day, in 1864, when the United States government forced them to leave.

Kit Carson is waiting to
*   march against the foe.*
To meet and crush bold
*   Johnny Navajo.*
Johnny Navajo,
*   O Johnny Navajo,*
We'll first chastise, then
*   civilize*
Bold Johnny Navajo.

AS they were being marched 350 miles to the reservation in Fort Sumner, New Mexico, Dinétah burned. Anyone who fell behind was shot. "Mercy" was an unknown word.

EVERY Navajo knows of the "The Long Walk" and marks time from that monstrous event. No one can understand the story of the Navajo without grasping the depravity of this debacle.

HUNDREDS of deaths and four years later, the People returned to Dinétah. They were not free, but they were home.

SCHOOLS opened on the reservation, but many children were sent away to boarding schools to separate them completely from their native culture. *Navajos should learn English,* the Anglos demanded. The traditional language of the People was forbidden.

"**THEY'D** make you stand in front of the classroom," one elder recalled, "and tell you to stick out your tongue, and then they'd whip it with a wooden ruler just for speaking our language." Yet there would come a day when that language would inspire admiration rather than ridicule.

DECEMBER 7, 1941

WHEN Japanese bombs thundered down on Pearl Harbor, the 20th century had yet to catch up with the desert-dwelling Navajo. Soon enough, the People would become a bargaining chip in World War II, for they possessed an enviable asset: their language.

THE Japanese were ingeniously successful at cracking wartime codes. Civil engineer Philip Johnston, an Anglo missionary's son who had grown up with the Navajo, thought of a way to thwart them: encode an entire language. You can break a code, but you must learn a language.

APART from its beauty, the Navajo tongue is unique, enormously difficult, and unwritten. It could become, Johnston argued, the ultimate unbreakable wartime code.

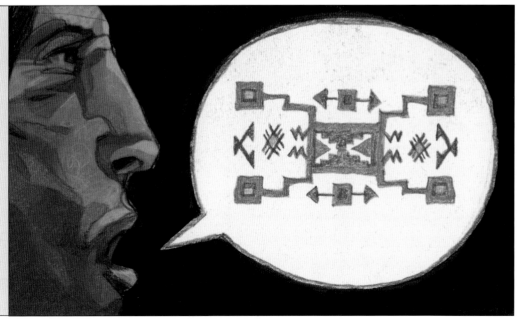

TO convince skeptics, the Marines proposed a test between Marine signalmen and four Navajo servicemen. The signalmen took an hour to transmit and receive the coded texts. For the Navajos, a mere 40 seconds elapsed.

SUDDENLY, bilingual Navajos had become valuable. Recruited into the military that had once sought to destroy their ancestors, the "code talkers" were born.

THE platoon of 29 code talkers first had to memorize 211 words—later expanded to more than 400. The Navajo men used words in their own language for terms that had no Navajo equivalents. For *Navy*, code talkers would say the Navajo word representing each letter: *Nesh-chee* (nut, for N), *wol-la-chee* (ant, for A); *a-keh-di-glini* (victor, for V), and *tsah-as-dzoh* (yucca, for Y).

TALKING CODE

Match the Navajo word
(and its coded meaning)
with its English translation
represented by the
pictures at the right.

1) ne-he-mah (America)

2) lo-tso (battleship)

3) a-ye-shi (bombs)

4) hash-kay-gi-na-tah
   (commander)

5) ca-lo (destroyer)

6) da-he-tih-hi (fighter plane)

7) ne-as-jah (observer plane)

8) son-na-kih (major general)

9) chay-da-gahi (tank)

SHARK

OUR MOTHER

OWL

HUMMINGBIRD

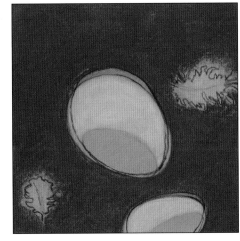

EGGS

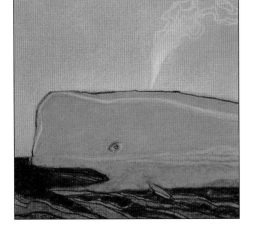

WHALE

TORTOISE

TWO STARS

WAR CHIEF

LIKE the great "winged rock" called Shiprock that figures so prominently in Navajo stories and that drew their ancestors to Dinétah, code talkers were carried away across the Pacific by other vessels.

THE work of the code talkers cloaked the American troops' movements wherever they went. Accounts from Japanese newspapers described people's confusion. To them, Navajo words sounded like "a strange earful of gurgling noises ... resembling the call of a Tibetan monk and the sound of a hot water bottle being emptied."

21

THE double-encrypted code was so sophisticated that even Navajos who were not code talkers couldn't understand it. And yet speed and accuracy were absolutely critical.

A single letter out of place could spell death to a whole platoon. At Iwo Jima, 6 code talkers worked feverishly during this month-long campaign to send 800 messages—without an error.

TRAVELING deep into enemy territory, the Navajo code talkers brought Dinétah with them in the form of corn pollen. Carrying it in medicine bags, the pollen reminded them of home. They would need that comfort as death rained down around them.

THE Navajo were a part of every assault the U.S. Marines conducted in the Pacific from 1942 to 1945. According to Major Howard Connor, a Marine signal officer, "Were it not for the Navajos, the Marines would never have taken Iwo Jima."

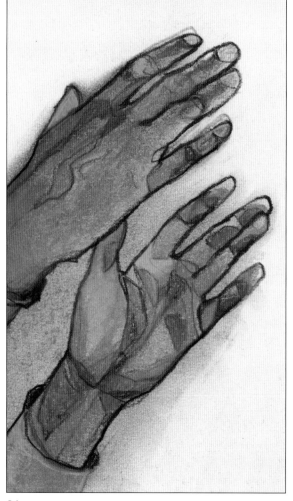

WHEN Americans cheered the Allied victory at war's end, the code talkers were sworn to silence about their heroic battlefield activities. The code itself was classified for security purposes. Not even their closest relatives could know what the code talkers had achieved in the war. But by 1968, new technologies and encryption methods led the military to lift the ban. The secret was out. Navajo code-talking would never be used again.

At long last, the heroic story of the People could be told.

ENDNOTES

According to the National Museum of the American Indian, here is a list of the American Indian Code Talkers' languages and the known number of tribal members who served during World War II. There were at least two code talkers from each tribe.

Assiniboine	Menominee
Cherokee	Muscogee/Creek and Seminole
Chippewa/Oneida (17)	Navajo (about 420)
Choctaw (8)	Pawnee
Comanche (17)	Sac and Fox/Meskwaki (19)
Hopi (11)	Sioux—Lakota and Dakota
Kiowa	

On the morning of December 7, 1941, hundreds of Japanese fighter planes attacked the naval base at Pearl Harbor in Honolulu, Hawaii. They destroyed 8 battleships and killed more than 2,000 American soldiers and sailors. The day after the assault, president Franklin D. Roosevelt asked Congress to declare war on Japan. More than two years after other countries had entered the conflict of World War II, the U.S. finally took to the battlefields of Europe, Asia, and Africa.

Iwo Jima, a tiny Pacific island, was of great tactical importance late in the war (February 1945). The Japanese were determined to control it. After a bloody battle in which nearly 7,000 American soldiers were killed and 18,000 wounded, U.S. forces defeated 22,000 Japanese soldiers and captured the island.

President Ronald Reagan declared August 14, 1982, National Navajo Code Talkers Day. But it wasn't until 2001 that the original 29 Navajo men were recognized with Congressional Gold Medals for their invaluable contributions that helped turn the tide of World War II.

ARTIST'S NOTES

page 7: Frontiersman and Indian agent Kit Carson was respected by some American Indian tribes but vilified by others, especially the Navajo, after his enforcement of the 1860s campaigns against the Apache and Navajo.

pages 9, 26–27: Under the banner of the American flag, the Navajo suffered greatly in the 1860s. Yet 80 years later, they were fighting under the U.S. flag in World War II. When asked why, they responded, "It's OUR country."

pages 11 & 12: These two portraits represent the profound difference between reservation life and boarding school life. Page 11 is a reflection of the Navajo belief that life is the freedom of a big circle. The boxed-in figure on page 12 symbolizes the government's preference at that time for containing and restricting native peoples.

page 15: To visually represent the beauty and complexity of the Navajo language, I used an element of a traditional Navajo storm pattern blanket design.

pages 20 & 29: The great "winged rock" in both scenes is Shiprock, a rock formation that is a notable landmark in northwestern New Mexico and important in Navajo mythology.

pages 26–27: Joe Rosenthal's 1945 Pulitzer Prize–winning photograph *Raising the Flag on Iwo Jima* directly inspired this image.

page 23: Another ceremonial blanket design suggests the sacred value of the corn pollen carried by the code talkers for comfort and protection.

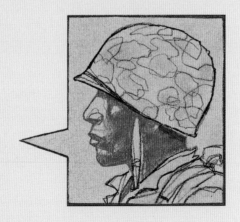

SELECTED BIBLIOGRAPHY

Aaseng, Nathan. *Navajo Code Talkers*. New York: Walker, 1992.

Greenberg, Henry, and Georgia Greenberg. *Power of a Navajo: Carl Gorman; the Man and His Life*. Santa Fe: Clear Light, 1996.

Holiday, Samuel, and Robert S. McPherson. *Under the Eagle: Samuel Holiday, Navajo Code Talker*. Norman: University of Oklahoma Press, 2013.

Holm, Tom. *Code Talkers and Warriors: Native Americans and World War II*. New York: Chelsea House, 2007.

McClain, Sally. *Navajo Weapon: The Navajo Code Talkers*. Tucson, Ariz.: Rio Nuevo, 2001.

Nez, Chester. *Code Talker*. With Judith Schiess Avila. New York: Berkley / Penguin, 2011.